To Julius and Gertrude, our canine family members

Photography: Tom Caravaglia, 50.
Fritz Prenzel, 9. Ron Reagan, 29, 43.
Vincent Serbin, front endpapers, 14, 17,
21, 27, 31, 33, 36 (top), 47, 55. Sally
Anne Thompson, 13, 15, 19, 20, 22, 23,
26, 38, 39, 40, 45, 51, 52, 53, 57.

A Beginner's Guide to
Dog Care

Written by
Clarke Fuller

Contents

1.
Introduction

This little book will introduce you to the general care requirements for dogs. Since most people get a dog as a puppy, we've thought it best and most convenient to emphasize puppy care. Once a dog is a year or 18

The dog has long been man's best friend.

months old its care becomes more or less routine and very basic—feeding, grooming, and veterinary care. The best way to learn to care for a dog is to raise a puppy.

The subject of dogs is as big as a pup is small. Yet, despite the dozens of breeds—and the countless types of mongrels, curb-mutts—all dogs and puppies are pretty much the same. They're lovable. They're cute. They're excusably mischievous. They're fun. Puppies are living little teddy bears for toddlers and a source of merriment and wonder for the grown-ups. Where is there a better spirit-lifter-upper than the pup? Where a truer friend than a dog?

The many, many kinds of dogs

Although one Latin name (*Canis familiaris*) covers all dogs for the purpose of zoology, there are so many varieties with so many different histories and background that it seems almost impossible to believe that they are all related. Look at a Chihuahua and then at a Great Dane. Some difference! Why? Because man bred them into these strange and wondrous shapes intentionally. He wanted to create dogs suitable for the various purposes for which he required them—hunting, guarding, herding, fighting, showing, or just as friends and companions.

Picking the right puppy

How can you possibly pick one puppy from a litter of playful, tailwagging little fellows? Take your time. Shop around. A well-kept kennel or a clean pet shop carrying a large variety of dogs will give you an opportunity to make a good selection. Price will enter into it, of course.

There are many dog breeds from which to choose. This Old English Sheepdog requires a great deal of grooming attention, so consider this before you make your selection.

Pedigreed dogs cost much more than mongrels, and the longer their pedigree the higher the price.

Many people prefer the pedigreed pup because they know what he will look like when he grows up. Mongrels may resemble neither of their parents—but so what? They are always just as faithful and loyal, even if they do make it hard to guess how big they'll grow or what they'll look like.

Unless you intentionally plan to breed dogs, forget about which sex is better. People who own males insist that their dogs make the better pets; people who own females are equally certain about theirs. There are too many differences in the personalities of the individual dogs to be able to generalize. Additionally, most pet dogs will be neutered or "fixed" when they mature. Neutering helps make the household pet a friendlier, more stable, and even possibly longer-lived animal.

Look for an active puppy, one who rolls and romps over his brothers and sisters. This is not a hard-bound rule, however. A sad-eyed shy pup, once he's out of his litter and getting your undivided attention, may blossom out beautifully.

Registration papers: If you pay for a purebred dog make sure that you get his pedigree papers and an application signed by the breeder that you will need to register your puppy with the American Kennel Club. The people who sell you your pet will help you make out these important forms. If your dog is not registered it cannot participate in dog shows nor can its offspring be registered.

Because of its small size, the Pekingese is especially suited to apartment living.

Outside the U.S.A. other national kennel clubs have their own rules about registering and showing dogs. Even in the U.S.A. certain breeds (Coonhounds, Eskimo, etc.) are registered by a different club, the United Kennel Club.

Bringing the new puppy home

Bring him home in the daytime, in the morning if possible. This gives him a chance to become acquainted with his new surroundings before it's time to go to bed.

His new quarters should be waiting his arrival. His bed can be in a wire cage or a wooden box with sides high enough to keep him in and drafts out. Put a flat washable cushion or an old folded blanket at one end of the box and some newspaper at the other.

Airline pet carriers are often used as homes for new puppies. They are sturdy, easily available, can be used as carrying cages for trips to the vet, and with small dogs they rapidly become a permanent "house" and retreat.

The first night give him warm milk just before he goes to bed. Make up your mind he is going to be a little lonesome for his mother. When he starts to whimper, an occasional firm "Quiet" will silence him. Other stratagems include a hot water or thermos bottle and a ticking alarm clock wrapped in towels to remind him of the warm bodies and beating hearts of his brothers and sisters.

2.
Feeding

Before leaving the seller of your puppy, have him give you a list of what the puppy has been eating, even to the brand names. Continue this same diet for about a week to avoid upsetting his digestion. Then make

Puppies look forward to their meals with great enthusiasm.

The nutritional needs of puppies, in this case a Shetland Sheepdog, change as the dog matures.

Proper diet and exercise are important for all dogs. If ever you are in doubt about your dog's health, consult a veterinarian.

changes gradually, adding a little bit of the new food to the old, until after a few days he's on the new diet one hundred percent.

The following diet would be suitable for a puppy of medium size. It was constructed before the days of canned and packaged foods, so it isn't really practical for most dog owners, but it serves to remind the owner of just what goes into a dog's diet. Today the meat comes from cans and the toast from bags of kibble, while vitamins are added to almost all foods by the manufacturer. Many dogs do not digest milk well, so cottage cheese is often substituted.

Age 2 months

Morning: 5 to 6 tablespoonfuls milk; 3 to 4 tablespoonfuls cereal. Noon: 1 to 2 heaping tablespoonfuls raw ground meat. Afternoon: Repeat morning feeding. Evening: Repeat noon feeding. Late evening: 5 to 6 tablespoonfuls milk. 1 to 2 teaspoonfuls cod-liver oil twice a day.

Age 3 months

Increase amounts per feeding—according to puppy's growth and capacity. Gradually eliminate afternoon and late evening feeding.

Age 4 months

Morning: ½ to 1 cup milk; 4 to 8 tablespoonfuls cereal. Noon: 4 to 8 heaping tablespoonfuls meat. Evening: 4 to 8 heaping tablespoonfuls cooked mashed vegetables. 3 to 5 teaspoonfuls cod-liver oil twice a day.

Nylabone® is the perfect "pooch pacifier" and the safest bone for your dog to chew on. It channels his chewing tendencies into something constructive, and it helps clean the teeth and massage the gums.

17

Age 5 months

Increase amounts per feeding.

Age 6 months

Morning: ¾ to 1½ cups milk; ¾ to 1½ cups cereal. Noon: ½ to 1 cup meat; ½ to 1 cup cereal. Evening: 1 to 2 cups meat; ½ to 1 cup cereal; ½ to 1 cup vegetables or table scraps. 1½ to 2 tablespoonfuls cod-liver oil twice a day, or vitamin concentrate.

Age 7 months

Gradually eliminate noon meal for the 30-pound dog.

**Age 8 months
(Smaller Breed)**

Morning: 1½ cups milk: 4 slices buttered toast, or 8 tablespoonfuls cereal. Evening: 2 cups meat; 5 slices toast, or ½ cup cereal; 1 cup vegetables, or table scraps. 1½ tablespoonfuls cod-liver oil twice a day, or vitamin concentrate.

(Larger Breed)

Morning: 2 cups milk; 2 cups cereal. Noon: 1½ cups meat; 1 cup cereal. Evening: 2 cups meat; 1 cup cereal or toast; 1 cup vegetables, or table scraps. 2½ tablespoonfuls cod-liver oil or vitamin concentrate.

Age 9 months

Gradually eliminate noon meal for 50-pound dog and start to reduce amount of food.

Children and puppies are so natural together.

Age 10 months

Morning: 1 to 1½ cups milk; 2 to 3 slices toast, or ½ to ¾ cups cereal. Evening: 1½ to 2½ cups meat; 1 cup cereal, or 4 to 6 slices toast; 1 cup vegetables, or table scraps. 1½ to 3 tablespoonfuls cod-liver oil twice a day, or vitamin concentrate.

Age 11 months

Continue 10 months' diet for 30 pound dog, or eliminate morning feeding. Further reduce amount of food for 50-pound dog, or eliminate morning meal.

Ages 12 to 14 months

1¼ to 1¾ cups meat; 1¼ to 1½ cups cereal or toast; 1¼ to 1¾ cups vegetables or table scraps. 1½ to 3 ta-

Labrador Retrievers are available in three colors—black, yellow, and chocolate.

blespoonfuls cod-liver oil twice a day until warm weather, or vitamin concentrate.

With today's packaged and prepared foods feeding a puppy is easy. Your veterinarian will probably provide you with a simplified diet to follow, and in a few months your dog will let you know his preferences. Many people like to feed adult dogs a mixture of canned and kibbled (cereal) foods plus snacks. Many dogs do better on two meals a day than on one larger meal.

Dogs—including puppies—like to chew and should be provided with "chewies." Nylabone nylon dog bones are safe, long-lasting chews in a world where rawhide chews are often cured with arsenic. Many types of chewies are available at your pet shop. **Don't feed your**

Young puppies need soft foods which are more easily digested. This youngster, a Chow Chow, seems to have gotten his fill!

dog fish or chicken bones; they can splinter and choke him. Avoid spicy foods and sweets; they spoil a dog for other foods, providing useless calories with little nutritive value.

Don't give your dog scraps from the table—at least not while you're dining, and always place them in his own bowl kept in its usual place.

Don't forget plenty of water. Keep it fresh, rinsing and refilling the bowl (don't just add to it) at least twice a day.

If you don't see the pup you want in a pet shop, perhaps the pet dealer can contact a breeder of the particular dog breed you want.

3.
Training

Housebreaking

This should begin the day you bring your puppy home. With persistence, housebreaking can be accomplished in

This Sheltie is being offered a tidbit as a reward for learning the "beg" trick.

from two to four weeks with only an occasional lapse for a short time after that.

The puppy will usually want to relieve himself about ten minutes after eating. If at all possible, take him outdoors at this time. Until he is about six months old it may be necessary to walk him five times a day. On these walks he will probably show a preference for a spot that other dogs have used. When he does, walk him to this particular place every time you take him out, and he will soon associate the outings with the idea of relieving himself and will usually do so promptly when he gets to his preferred spot. When he has relieved himself, praise him highly and take him right back inside to impress on him that this is the purpose of the walk.

Paper training

Spread out newspapers in some spot you have designated as his comfort station. Shortly after he has eaten, take him there and stay with him until he has had his movement, and then praise him highly.

Remove the soiled newspapers and replace them with clean ones, but leave one of the scented old papers on top. Or, if you prefer, purchase at your pet shop one of the several housebreaking aids that are made for this purpose. The odor reminds the puppy of what the papers are for.

When you begin paper training, spread the newspapers over a wide area. You will discover that he will return to a preferred spot. Gradually reduce the spread of papers until you have only a few thicknesses spread where he wants them. Scold him firmly when he does make a mistake, then carry him to his comfort station. At the

If you buy a purebred dog, such as this Sheltie (Shetland Sheepdog), chances are he will be housebroken. Be sure to inquire about this before you purchase the dog.

An Airedale learning to "heel." Training should begin when a dog is young.

Labrador Retrievers are strong swimmers and were originally bred to re-trieve waterfowl.

most, his punishment should be a smack across the rump with a rolled-up newspaper. Scrub the soiled spot immediately with vinegar or ammonia diluted in warm water. This will kill any odor which might attract him back.

To make the transition from newspapers inside to useing the great outdoors exclusively, take along a fold of soiled newspaper—or a can of the commercial housebreaking aid—when you walk him. Spread this on the spot you prefer him to use, and if and when he does, praise him profusely. Praise yourself too because you've both done a good job.

Good manners

Thou Shalt Not Sit on Furniture: If he has a comfortable spot of his own, your dog is less likely to choose yours. A stern "No" emphasized with the crack of a rolled-up newspaper will point out his mistake. He'll catch on quickly if you keep at it. Dog repellent sprays are also useful for keeping dogs off furniture. They smell bad to dogs but not to you and are harmless when sprayed on upholstery.

Thou Shalt Not Jump on People: When your half-grown puppy jumps you should throw him back by grabbing his front paws and flinging him away, at the same time saying "No" sharply. Or try raising your knee as he rears up so that he bumps against it. If he won't learn this way, try stepping lightly but sharply on his back feet.

Thou Shalt Not Chew Our Belongings: A puppy is anxious to test his new teeth on almost anything, so give him sturdy items of his own such as Nylabone to chomp on. Approval or disapproval can be shown in your voice. Tell him "Good dog" when he chews on his own things, but say a firm "No!" when he chews on yours, accompanying it with a snap of your newspaper for emphasis. Make sure that everyone in the family does this consistently.

Thou Shalt Not Bark: If your puppy yelps while you're away, your neighbors will let you know about it fast. Their complaints are justified, so take the trouble to break your little monster of this habit while there's still time. Make believe you're going away, but wait quietly outside the door. The chances are he'll start to howl as soon as he thinks you've gone. Shout "No, No, No!" as if you meant it and rush back inside, scolding him fiercely and making a great display of displeasure. A few

Many people keep their dogs outdoors in good weather. If this is the case, do provide a dog house where your friend can spend time resting.

lessons like this before his bad habit becomes ingrained will teach him that the only thing that results from yelping and barking is a very angry master.

A dog who barks a warning is a valuable companion, but a yapper who barks at any and everything is a nuisance unless he is taught to stop on command.

Simple obedience training

While manners and housebreaking should be taught to your puppy from the day he enters your home, simple obedience commands like those given here can wait until he's at least six months old. The need for patience when it comes to dog training cannot be overemphasized. With patience goes persistence. Repeat and repeat the lesson until it has been learned.

Walking on a leash: Teaching a puppy this is not difficult, but before you start, get him used to wearing a collar or choke chain and leash. Get him used to the collar or choker by letting him wear it around the house for a longer time each day.

After a couple of days like this, take him on his first walk. Call him to your side and as you step out say "Heel." This is an obedience command he will have to learn later so he might just as well get used to it from the start. He will want to drag behind or rush ahead, and he will plunge and pull against the lead. Continue your walk, however, pulling him along with you, repeating "Heel." He will quickly learn that it is useless to struggle and more comfortable to come along than to be dragged. When he ceases to struggle, pet him and reward him.

These Irish Setter littermates are about the right age to begin simple obedience training.

Commands

"Come": Attach a light check cord at least 20 feet long to his collar—clothesline works fine. Allow your pup to have a short romp, then, when his attention is attracted elsewhere, call him by name and give the command "Rover, come!". If he responds, pat him, reward him with a treat, and allow him to continue his romp, repeating the call at intervals. Before long he will refuse to come when ordered. Grasp the end of the taut cord, repeat the command, and give the cord a sharp jerk. He will probably try to resist, but keep giving the command; a few sharp jerks will probably bring him to you. If they don't, pull him in, but reward him anyway.

However badly a puppy misbehaves, never scold him when he comes to you. A dog must always feel that when you say "Come" something good is going to happen.

Walking on a leash is one of the first lessons your dog should learn.

"Sit": With your pup in front of you or by your side, hold the leash taut in your right hand and give the command "Sit." At the same time lean over and with your left hand press down on his rump until he is sitting. He may want to lie down or flop over on his side. Don't let him. Straighten him out with your left hand on his flank or use the leash to pull him up into a Sit. Then slip a treat into his mouth and praise him. Repeat this routine several times, always rewarding him when he responds. Soon he will associate the command with the pressure and anticipate it before he is touched.

"Down": Once he sits on command, it is not difficult to teach "Down." With one hand hold him by the collar, give the command "Down," and press down on his rump with the other. When he is sitting, use the right hand to pull his front feet out from under him while you still press down with your left hand. Another way is to

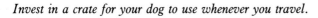

Invest in a crate for your dog to use whenever you travel.

pass the leash under your shoe and hold it taut with your right hand while pressing down on his shoulder with your left, at the same time commanding "Down." Give the command "Up" and take a step or two forward when you want him to rise. Repetition of this will soon teach your dog to go down on all fours at the command, and with the second command "Stay" remain there for long periods.

Puppies love to jump up on furniture. You must break them of this habit early before it gets out of hand.

"Stay": This command is an extension of "Sit" or "Down." Command him to "Sit" or "Down." Face the dog and order him to "Stay." Back slowly away, admonishing him with your upraised finger. If he breaks, give him a sharp "No!" Lay the leash on the ground pointing from him to you as you back away. Keep repeating "Stay" or "No" according to his reaction. At each lesson move farther away until there is an open space between you and the loop of the leash. If he stays only momentarily at first, still praise and reward him when you call him to you.

"Heeling": This is the correct way to walk a mature dog. The loop of the leash is held in your right hand and the thong passes across your body to the dog, who is sitting on your left; you control the slack of the leash with your left hand, shortening or lengthening it as the case may be. Say clearly, "Rover, heel!" and start out with your left foot. When the dog strains ahead, jerk back sharply with your left hand but then let the leash slacken instantly. The jerk is what does it. It makes him momentarily uncomfortable and he quickly learns that if he walks correctly at your left knee there will be no jerk. Keep walking, keep jerking when needed, and keep repeating "Heel." Some trainers use a rolled-up tube of newspaper to tap the dog on the nose whenever they say "Heel," but this is probably not necessary. Patting your left leg often helps, however. Remember to praise him on each return to position. Fifteen minutes a day, twice a day. You'll be surprised how quickly he learns.

"Shake hands": Puppies paw at each other in play. Your pup will paw at you. Fine. Grab his paw and shake. Wrong paw? Yes, since most pups extend the paw nearest the hand you're using. With the pup in the Sit position, push against his right shoulder with your left hand. As his foot comes up, take the paw in your right hand, shake, then reward. Keep repeating the command "Shake hands" as you rehearse him in the action. After he has learned this well, teach him to shake left-handed by a slightly different command like "Other paw."

Because of their intelligence and small size, Pekingese (above) *are very trainable. Labradors* (left) *enjoy a good game of "fetch" out-of-doors.*

Many dog owners like to purchase a pair of puppies so that they will keep each other company while the family is away during working or school hours.

"Beg": Don't attempt this trick until the pup's back is strong. Wait until the smaller breed dog is at least six months old; it should not be attempted with the larger breeds until they are nine months or a year old. Work in the corner of the room. Hold the dog's favorite toy above his head until he has risen on his hind feet. Back him into the corner so that he has the wall angle to help support him. With your free hand take one of his paws and balance him back on his haunches. Command him to "Beg" while you are doing this. Reward him immediately. After a few times, just steady him with one finger. When he has learned to beg in this manner, try commanding him to "Beg" when he's sitting square on the ground. He'll recognize the word but the situation will be different. His front feet are down. Raise him up gently. He'll be expecting something like this so his backbone will quickly stiffen. Repeat—praise—reward.

Learning to shake hands.

4.
Grooming

A dog deserves a little special attention at least once a day. This is a good time to take care of his coat and to check his eyes, ears, nose, teeth, and claws.

Bathing out-of-doors should only be done on warm days.

After his bath, this young Miniature Schnauzer has his collar put in place.

Brushing: Use a soft bristle brush for a young pup. As he matures you'll need a stiffer brush or curry-comb, and if he's got a long, shaggy coat, a steel comb and wire brush will be needed to untangle the snarls. First, brush with the grain—or growth—of the hair to clean the surface coat. Second, brush stiffly against the grain to clean out the undercoat and massage the skin. Finally, brush the hair back to its original position. Use the comb to tease out mats and snarls from long-haired dogs, using a few teeth at one end to work them out. Use the comb, too, for ear fringes, beards, and feathered tails.

Bathing: Dogs should not be bathed except when necessary; never more than once a month, and not even then unless there's some special reason. Choose a warm place and put several inches of lukewarm water into a fairly deep tub. Use a washrag without soap on his head and ears. Then, using dog soap or shampoo, lather him over from neck to tail, back to paws, including his under body. Do not let any suds get in his nose, eyes, or ears. After soaping him down and rubbing into the skin, rinse it completely. A shampoo hose attachment or a sprinkling-can will come in handy here. It is important to get out every bit of soap.

Then, before you lift him from the tub, wrap him in a big towel. This will protect you from his natural instinct to shake himself dry. When he is as dry as you can get him, let him romp around in a warm room that is free from drafts. Dry shampoos that are sprayed or wiped on and wiped off are available at your pet store. They are easy to use and highly practical in winter or at times when a tub bath is out of the question.

Care of the eyes: If your dog has been running

through high weeds and grass, you may find pollen or seeds under the lid. Irritated eyes can be treated with a dog eyewash available at pet stores. Don't hesitate to see the vet if any inflammation persists. To clean mucus from the corners of the eyes use only a cotton swab dipped in warm water.

Care of the ears: His hearing will be extra-keen if his ears are kept clean and healthy. Do not use soap and water on them, however. Use a cotton swab dipped in peroxide or mineral oil. Be gentle. Avoid probing. Here, too, you may prefer to use a commercially prepared dog earwash that might even contain a mite medication.

Care of the teeth: Puppies and young dogs who are allowed to gnaw on hard items usually keep their own teeth clean. Many owners brush an adult dog's teeth with a normal toothbrush and toothpaste. If greatly discolored, his teeth can be bleached with hydrogen peroxide, which also helps cut down on gum infections.

Care of the feet: Examine the feet carefully after each romp. Prompt attention should be given to any cut in the pads. If the nails are allowed to grow too long, they may tear off. If they are kept trimmed or the dog is given exercise on hard pavements to keep them worn down, there should be no trouble from this source. Tar and gum may be removed from his feet with acetone or nail polish remover.

To keep nails clipped you will find a dog nail clipper most useful. When clipping a dog's nails be overly careful not to cut into the quick and draw blood. If this does happen the blood flow can usually be stopped with a styptic powder.

Good health in dogs does not happen by accident. Owners must keep a constant check on their charges to ensure all is well. Nails need to be trimmed periodically; ears, eyes, and teeth need to be checked; and so forth.

Spraying for fleas is part of canine care. Not only the dog, but his environment as well, must be treated whenever fleas are suspected.

5.
First Aid

Lively little pups and most adult dogs have good resilient bones and constitutions that are to be admired. They are also filled with unbounded enthusiasm and uncontrolled energy at times. However, there may come

With practice, pilling your dog can be done easily.

an occasion when you will have to render first aid to your dog. Here are a few of the possibilities that you should be prepared for.

The first thing you should *not* do is to rush to the injured animal and gather him up in your arms. An injured dog is in pain and he may snap at and even bite those he loves. If he is a small dog obtain a blanket or a heavy piece of cloth, fold it into double thickness, and drop it over the injured animal. Then gather it around him and pick him up. Do not do this, however, if it is obvious that a bone has been broken.

A dog of a large breed may need an emergency muzzle. Take a strip of strong cloth about a yard long and a few inches wide. Make a loop in the center and slip this over his jaws, tightening the knot under his chin. Then bring the ends back over his head and tie them securely behind his ears.

Shock: A badly injured dog may go into shock, which should be treated immediately. Shock symptoms are a weak but rapid pulse, lethargy, and weakness. The victim is conscious but seems unaware of what is going on. Keep the dog warm. Put a blanket over him and if possible take him indoors. Give him a stimulant. Coffee is fine; add cream, sugar, and a pinch of salt to fortify it. Smelling salts can be used too.

Broken bones: Puppies have such flexible bones that a fracture is rare, but accidents do happen, especially during falls and jumps. In large and older dogs the bones may be more brittle. If a leg is broken, keep it as straight as possible. If the bone has pierced the skin, make a splint out of a stick, attaching it to the leg by

In multi-dog households, disease can run rampant if the animals are not immunized regularly. Check with a veterinarian about a routine immunization program.

tape above and below the break. This will help to prevent the jagged bone from cutting a blood vessel. Pull the broken bone until the point no longer shows before splinting it. If the pelvis, a rib, or shoulder blade is broken, leave the dog alone until your veterinarian has been informed and has given you instructions. He will probably be able to set a broken rib or shoulder blade. A broken pelvis usually knits on its own or requires surgery.

Cuts and scratches: Even a small cut or scratch deserves antiseptic. You may wish to trim the hair around the wound to allow air to get to it. If the cut is in a paw, try holding the foot in a dish of sugar; this often causes a clot to form quickly. Dogs usually worry bandages off quickly, so if you put one on make sure that it's there to stay.

Accidental poisoning: A poisoned dog needs fast treatment. Don't lose precious time. First, empty his stomach. The easiest way is with hydrogen peroxide. Use the usual household strength (3%) diluted in half with water. Give him a teaspoonful of this mixture for every five pounds he weighs. Peroxide turns into oxygen and water in the stomach and is harmless, but it will cause the dog to vomit in about two minutes. After his stomach settles, give him Epsom salts, a teaspoonful in water. This will quickly empty the bowels.

If you know what the poison was and its antidote, you can give him that instead. Peroxide is an antidote for phosphorus, which is often used in rat poisons. Epsom salts is an antidote for lead poisoning, frequently caused by paint or paint odors. Ordinary photographer's "hypo" (sodium thiosulphate), a teaspoonful in water,

Dogs with long coats need extra grooming attention, as the hair can become tangled and matted. Occasionally check beneath the fur for parasites, abscesses, cuts, and the like.

is an antidote for arsenic. Use any or all of these if the poison is not known. If it is known, have someone phone the vet for instructions while you're giving the peroxide.

In the case of any poisoning, these emergency measures can be given while transporting the dog to the veterinarian or canine emergency hospital. Don't either withhold treatment until you see the vet or give treatment and then fail to see the vet. Many poisons act very fast, and many require rather elaborate treatments.

The ears on this German Shepherd Dog pup will become erect as he matures.

6.
Ailments

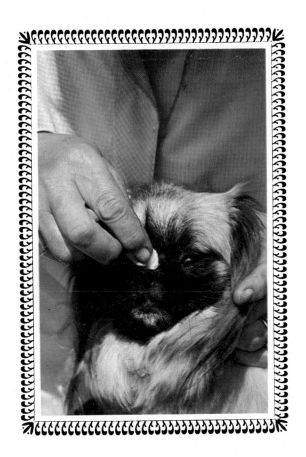

Your Veterinarian: Every dog owner should have a family veterinarian on whom he can call in times of need. Vets are needed not only when your dog is sick,

Gently wipe the corners of your dog's eyes with a cotton swab or cotton ball.

Dogs that are let outside should be supervised at all times or else placed in a fenced-in yard for their own protection.

The beloved St. Bernard is a rugged breed, able to withstand the cold temperatures of the Swiss Alps, where he has saved countless lives.

but to give regular examinations, periodic vaccinations, and yearly stool testing.

Skin diseases: Differentiating between eczema, mange, ringworm, and other skin diseases is a job for the professional. Small skin lesions may be treated with a mixture of equal parts of iodine and glycerine, applied daily. Many of the general purpose skin remedies available at your pet shop will prove effective. But if the problem persists, seek expert advice. *Caution:* Some skin diseases are transmissible to humans, so wash your hands thoroughly after handling a dog with a skin ailment.

Fleas: This problem must be attacked on two fronts. You have not only to rid your dog of the fleas and eggs infesting his body, you must also exterminate the eggs that have dropped off in his living and sleeping quarters. Use a good commercially prepared flea powder or aerosol spray, following the directions on the container. Then completely disinfect his quarters and bed. This done, go over the dog with a brush and fine-toothed comb to get rid of all the dead or dying parasites. Never neglect a dog's fleas or ticks; they can be the cause of serious skin trouble.

Ticks: These look like small purplish brown grapes. They cling to the dog's skin and even inside his ears. Touch them with a cotton swab dipped in alcohol or camphor. This loosens their hold and they can be plucked off with a tweezers. Grasp the tick firmly at the point where its head is embedded in the skin. If you pull a bit of skin with it, don't worry. This ensures that the tick's mouthparts have not been left behind to cause infection. Peroxide makes a good antiseptic.

Fleas generally are not a problem for dogs in winter, provided they are kept outdoors. Inside, however, where it is warm, fleas may be lurking.

Worms and worming: Even the best cared-for dogs are subject to worms. But not all worms are the same. There are roundworms, hookworms, whipworms, and tapeworms, to name a few. Each requires its own special treatment. So be sure of your worm and the medication if you decide to worm the dog yourself. It is best to have a stool sample from your dog checked by a vet each year. The vet can then prescribe the best and safest wormer. Common symptoms: Actual appearance of the worms or worm segments in the bowel movements or vomit. A "pot-belly," diarrhea, persistent vomiting, or running eyes and nose. Dragging the rump on the floor is sometimes an indication, but this usually means there is an accumulation of secreted matter in the dog's anal glands that should be removed; see your groomer or vet. Worming medicines are poisons and should be used very carefully. Always follow directions exactly.

Ear canker: A brown, waxy substance in your dog's ear may indicate trouble ahead. Clean out the ears with a cotton swab dipped in mineral oil, then bathe with a good medicated ear wash. If your pup continues to scratch his ears more than appears usual, see your vet for advice—the dog probably has an infection of microscopic ear mites.

Constipation: Diet is usually to blame, so change his menu. Give him more roughage: vegetables, kibble, dog biscuits. For fast relief, use milk of magnesia in a child's dose or, if you prefer, mineral oil straight or mixed in

When your dog steps out of his bath water, be prepared to get wet! By first covering the dog with a large turkish towel, you will avoid being splashed.

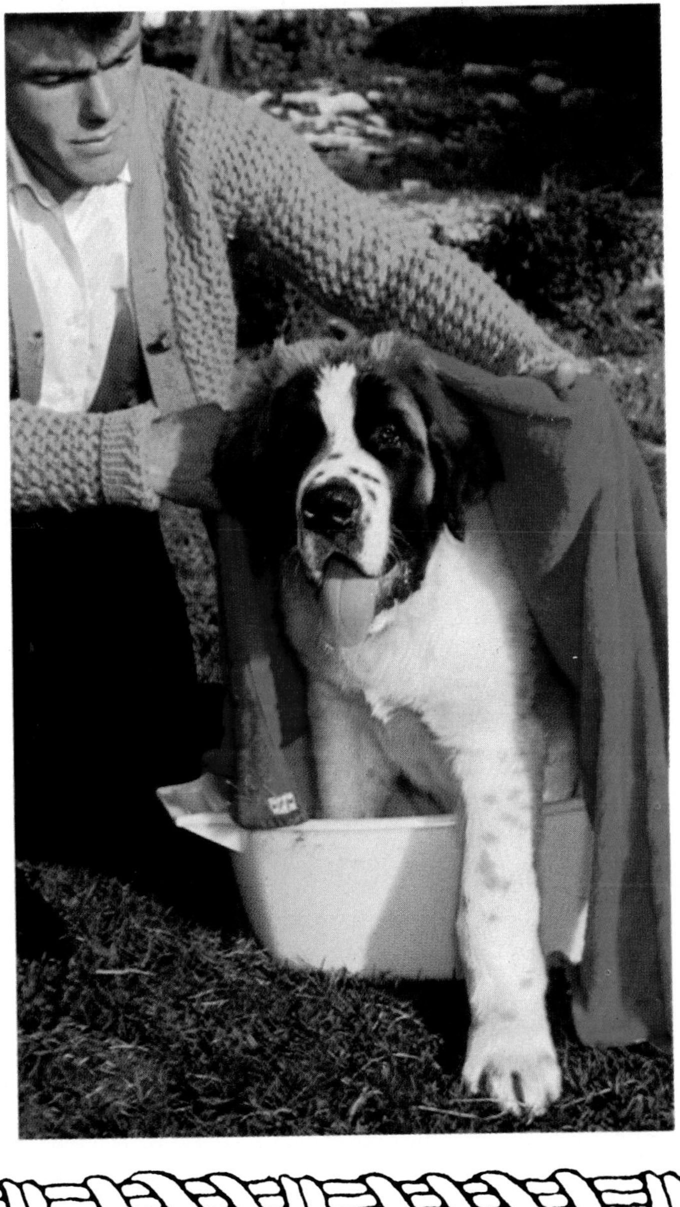

with his food. When the situation has been corrected, continue with the new diet; otherwise constipation will reappear.

Diarrhea: This too is frequently the result of bad diet, although it can be the symptom of something more serious. A teaspoonful of bismuth or magnesia laxatives for humans can be given every three hours. For severe cases, give the pup six ounces of black coffee laced with syrup. Remove all drinking water but allow him to lick ice cubes when he's thirsty. Rice may also help.

When a dog suffers from either constipation or diarrhea it is a good idea to check on whether he has been chewing some foreign matter. Wood, rubber, horsehair, plastic, wicker, foam rubber, paper, and carpet are some of the possible culprits. Prolonged bouts of either constipation or diarrhea are painful and may be signs of something more serious, so see your veterinarian if symptoms persist for more than a few days.

Fever: The dog's normal temperature, taken rectally, is 101 to 102.3°F. If it goes higher and stays high for 24 hours, consider it a danger signal. To take his temperature, place him on a table. Coat the bulb end of a rectal thermometer with petroleum jelly. Raise the dog's tail and insert the thermometer for half its length into the rectum. Leave it there for one to two minutes. After using it you will, of course, disinfect it immediately and shake it down.

Inoculations: Today the science of immunization has developed to a remarkable degree. Puppies can be given longlasting immunity when they are ten weeks old. Before that they can be given a temporary immunization. At the same time your vet gives your pup distemper shots, he will also immunize him against hepatitis and leptospirosis. We do not go into a description of these diseases because in their early stages the symptoms are similar. Only your veterinarian will be able to differentiate. Parvo-virus infections are deadly in puppies and may also present similar symptoms; inoculations are now available for this disease also.

Symptoms of distemper (Carre's disease), parvo, and several other diseases include elevated temperature, mucousy nose and/or eyes, loss of appetite, diarrhea, listlessness, frequent productive sneezing, vomiting, and a deep cough low in the abdomen as distinguished from a bronchial cough which is in the upper region. These symptoms alone are sufficient to suspect a serious disease although by themselves they do not support a positive diagnosis as many other less serious diseases will frequently cause the same symptoms. You must see your veterinarian.

Additional symptoms more characteristic of true distemper are photophobia or fear of light, a distinctive temperature curve, and conjunctivitis (eye inflammation). The puppy will hide in dimly lit areas and, when exposed to light, will squint and show his discomfort. Another distinctive symptom is the so-called diphasic, or saddle, curve of temperature. From the normal of 101 to 102.3°F the puppy's temperature will shoot up as high as 105°F on the fifth day after infection, followed by a drop to almost normal on the sixth. This is followed by a rise to 103 or 104°F, and it remains approximately that for the duration of the disease. Frequently, sores are seen on the stomach. The skin, when pinched, retains the crease, returning slowly to normal, in contrast to the skin of a healthy dog which snaps back.

In the early stages keep the puppy warm and check his temperature daily, keeping a written record. This will help your veterinarian make a positive diagnosis should the symptoms persist.

If symptoms persist you must, of course, contact your veterinarian. However, do not become unduly discouraged. While distemper, when it does appear, is extremely serious, antibiotics control the secondary infection and with good nursing there is a decent percentage of cures. Some, but by no means all, puppies are left with after-effects which might range from hardly noticeable to severe, but many do make a complete recovery. Should it turn out that it wasn't true distemper after all, but one of the other puppy ailments, the chances are good for a complete recovery.

Rabies: Almost every state and city requires vaccination for rabies at regular intervals. In the U.S.A. canine rabies is rare, but it does occur in dogs that can roam freely and meet skunks and raccoons.

Tracheobronchitis: This is frequently called "kennel cough" and is a common and contagious ailment of puppies and even adult dogs. The puppy seems normal in every way except for the dry hacking cough. Fortunately, the dog usually recovers without treatment, although the cough may persist for as long as six weeks. Dog cough medicines are available to ease the irritation in the throat, but for severe cases professional help will be needed.

Giving pills: To give pills, press the lips over the teeth with one hand to open the mouth. The pill can be pushed in with the index finger or index and middle finger. Hold the mouth closed for a few seconds and stroke the throat to promote swallowing.

Your dog may live quite a number of years and provide you with companionship in a way that most other pets cannot. Take care of him, using the suggestions in this book and the advice of a veterinarian, and you should enjoy a long life together.